GOAT:
Women in Sports

Mia Hamm

≫ Soccer GOAT ≪

 Gareth Stevens
PUBLISHING

HOT TOPICS

BY KRISTEN RAJCZAK NELSON

Please visit our website, www.garethstevens.com. For a free color catalog of all our high-quality books, call toll free 1-800-542-2595 or fax 1-877-542-2596.

Library of Congress Cataloging-in-Publication Data
Names: Rajczak Nelson, Kristen, author.
Title: Mia Hamm : soccer GOAT / Kristen Rajczak Nelson.
Description: Buffalo, N.Y. : Gareth Stevens Publishing, [2025] | Series:
   GOAT. Women in sports | Includes bibliographical references and index.
Identifiers: LCCN 2023034798 | ISBN 9781538293744 (library binding) | ISBN
   9781538293737 (paperback) | ISBN 9781538293751 (ebook)
Subjects: LCSH: Hamm, Mia, 1972–Juvenile literature. | Women soccer
   players–United States–Biography–Juvenile literature.
Classification: LCC GV942.7.H27 R35 2025 | DDC 796.334092
   [B]–dc23/eng/20230804
LC record available at https://lccn.loc.gov/2023034798

First Edition

Published in 2025 by
Gareth Stevens Publishing
2544 Clinton St
Buffalo, NY 14224

Copyright © 2025 Gareth Stevens Publishing

Designer: Leslie Taylor
Editor: Kristen Rajczak Nelson

Photo credits: Cover (photo) Jon Buckle/Alamy.com, (wreath) Igoron_vector_3D_ render/Shutterstock.com, (banner, cover & series background) RETHELD DESIGN IRI/ Shutterstock.com, (soccer icon) kosmofish/Shutterstockcom; p. 5 Johnmaxmena2/ https://commons.wikimedia.org/wiki/File:Mia_Hamm_1995_001_stl.jpg; pp. 7, 27 Global Sports Forum/Flickr.com; p. 9 Jonathan Larsen/Diadem Images/ Alamy.com; p. 11 Curt Gibbs/Flickr.com; pp. 13, 25 tony quinn/Alamy.com; p. 15 Daniel Motz/Alamy.com; p. 17 Matthew Ashton/Alamy.com; p. 19 momovieman/Flickr. com; pp. 21, 23 PCN Black/Alamy.com; p. 29 Rob Poetsch/Flickr.com.

Printed in the United States of America

Some of the images in this book illustrate individuals who are models. The depictions do not imply actual situations or events.

CPSIA compliance information: Batch #CSGS25: For further information contact Gareth Stevens, New York, New York at 1-800-542-2595.

Find us on

Contents

Soccer Great

Mia Hamm is more than the GOAT—greatest of all time—of women's soccer. She became the face of the sport! Her play with the U.S. women's national team (USWNT) in the World Cup and Olympics **inspired** millions of women and girls to play sports!

WHAT A STAR!

Mia appeared in a TV ad with basketball great Michael Jordan. They played different sports to see who was better!

One of Six

Mariel Margaret "Mia" Hamm was born on March 17, 1972, in Alabama. Mia had three sisters. When she was a kid, her parents, Bill and Stephanie, **adopted** her two brothers. Garrett was older than her. Martin was the youngest child.

WHAT A STAR!

Mia's family moved a lot for her dad's job in the U.S. Air Force. She grew up all over the United States and spent time in Italy.

Soccer Start

Mia first kicked a soccer ball as a young child living in Italy. When her family moved back to the United States, she continued to play soccer, now in Texas. She also played basketball. Mia played on a boys' football team too!

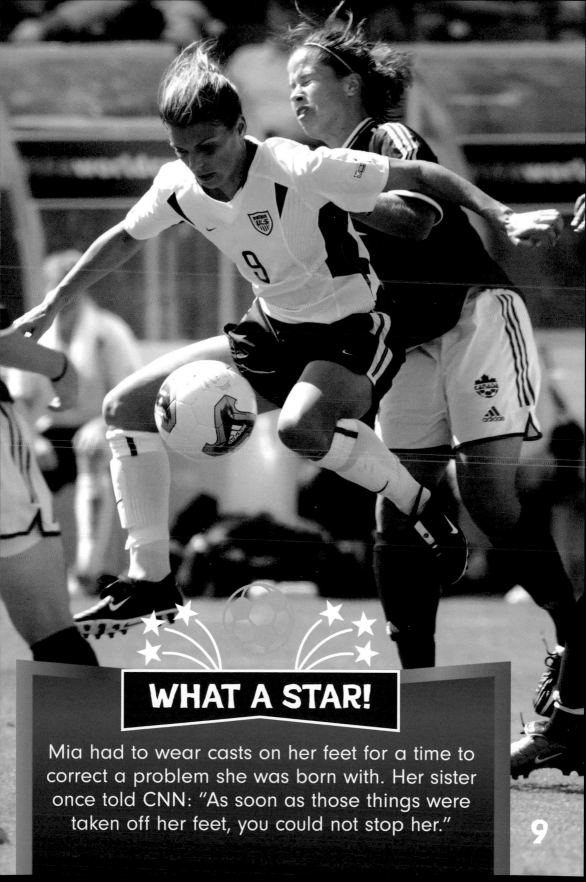

WHAT A STAR!

Mia had to wear casts on her feet for a time to correct a problem she was born with. Her sister once told CNN: "As soon as those things were taken off her feet, you could not stop her."

Just That Good

In 1986, Mia earned a spot on a girls' Olympic **development** soccer team. Mia was so good that she was moved up to the women's team. Then Mia made the USWNT! She had to move to Virginia to train with the team.

MIA

WHAT A STAR!

Mia was just 15 when she moved away from her
family, on her own, to train with the USWNT.

College Champ

The coach of the USWNT, Anson Dorrance, also coached the women's soccer team at the University of North Carolina at Chapel Hill (UNC). In 1989, Mia finished high school a year early and joined his team at UNC. The team won the **championship** that year!

KRISTINE LILLY

MIA

WHAT A STAR!

Mia played soccer at UNC with USWNT teammate Kristine Lilly, another women's soccer great.

The First World Cup

Mia and the UNC team won another championship in 1990! She took the 1991 season off from playing with UNC. Instead, she prepared for the first Women's World Cup with the USWNT! The team won, pushing Mia into the **international** spotlight.

1991 WORLD CUP

Mia was the youngest player on the USWNT during the 1991 World Cup.

Olympic Gold

Mia won two more championships with UNC in 1992 and 1993. Then women's soccer was added to the Olympics for the first time in 1996. Mia played with the USWNT to win gold! Mia became a hero to many who watched her play.

MIA

1996 OLYMPICS

WHAT A STAR!

In 1997, Mia's brother Garrett died. His illness inspired Mia to start the Mia Hamm Foundation in 1999. A foundation is a group that raises money and uses it to do good.

Mia Mania

Mia became one of the most well-known athletes—man or woman—in the United States! Mia didn't like being in the spotlight, but she wanted to help women's soccer grow. She understood her stardom brought in more fans.

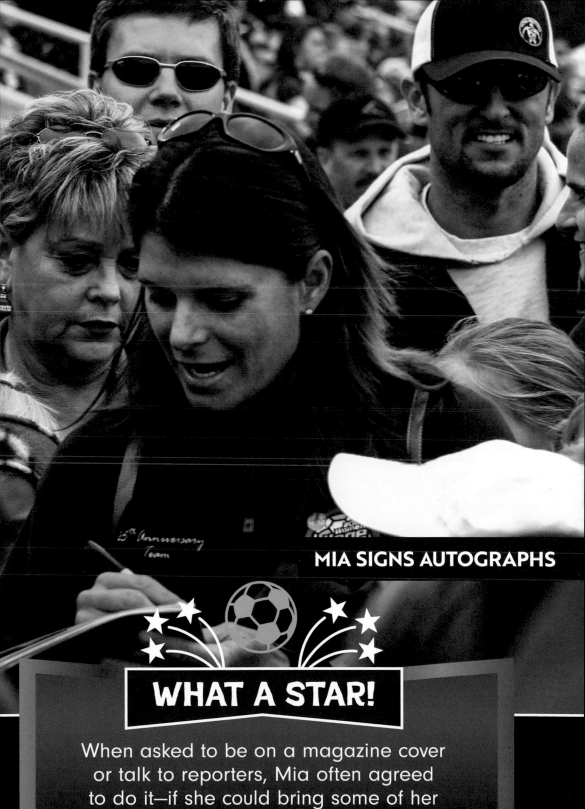

MIA SIGNS AUTOGRAPHS

WHAT A STAR!

When asked to be on a magazine cover or talk to reporters, Mia often agreed to do it—if she could bring some of her teammates along too!

Record Breaking

On March 22, 1999, Mia scored her 108th goal in international play. This broke the record for most career goals for any soccer player—man or woman! Mia added to this number and held this record until 2013, when Abby Wambach broke it.

WHAT A STAR!

After Abby broke the record, she said: "When I look in the mirror, I don't see a person who's made the kind of **impact** that Mia Hamm made on the game ... What she did for women's soccer can't be measured."

The '99 World Cup

The 1999 women's World Cup was held in California. More than 90,000 fans came to watch the final game. Mia had to take one of the shots in the shootout at the end of the game. Her goal helped the team win yet again!

MIA

WHAT A STAR!

In 2009, Mia said the 1999 World Cup win may have been the most important accomplishment of her **career**: "The event and championship meant so much to the sport of soccer in this country and for young girls all over the world."

Short-Lived League

The following year, Mia headed to the Olympics again. The USWNT won silver, losing to Norway in the final game. In 2001, Mia joined the Washington Freedom, a team in the new Women's United Soccer Association (WUSA).

WHAT A STAR!

The WUSA was the first American **professional** women's soccer league, or group of teams that play each other. It only lasted until 2003. Mia and the Freedom won the championship that year.

25

Retirement

In 2003, Mia announced she would retire, or stop playing professionally, after the 2004 Olympics. She finished her career on a high, winning another gold **medal** with the USWNT! Over 17 years, Mia played in 275 games, scored 158 goals, and earned 144 assists.

WHAT A STAR!

Mia is still part of the world of soccer. She works with the USWNT to this day and is a part owner of the Los Angeles Football Club!

Today, Mia works with her foundation to support programs for girls in sports. She also raises money for families dealing with the illness her brother died from. There's no question: Mia has used her greatness to make a difference!

WHAT A STAR!

Mia and her husband, baseball star Nomar Garciaparra, have three kids. Their twin daughters Ava and Grace were born in 2007. Their son Garrett was born in 2012.

Mia Hamm
HIGHLIGHTS

1987
Mia plays in her first game with the USWNT. She is only 15!

1989, 1990, 1992, 1993
Mia wins four NCAA championships with UNC.

1991
Mia and the USWNT win the first Women's World Cup.

1996
Mia wins her first Olympic gold medal with the USWNT.

1999
Mia wins another World Cup with the USWNT.

2000
Mia and the USWNT win an Olympic silver medal.

2004
Mia wins her second Olympic gold medal with the USWNT. She retires.

For More Information

BOOKS

Anderson, Josh. *Alex Morgan vs. Mia Hamm: Who Would Win?* Minneapolis, MN: Lerner Publications, 2024.

Mattern, Joanne. *Trailblazing Women in Soccer.* Chicago, IL: Norwood House Press, 2023.

WEBSITES

Mia Hamm
olympics.com/en/athletes/mia-hamm
Read more about Mia's career in the Olympics and beyond.

Mia Hamm Foundation
www.miafoundation.org
Find out about the goals of Mia's foundation and how she's working through it to help others.

Glossary

adopt: To make part of a family.

career: The job someone chooses to do for a long time.

championship: The honor given to the team that has shown itself to be the best in a sport.

development: The act or process of making better or more advanced over time.

impact: A powerful influence.

inspire: To make someone want to do something.

international: Including two or more countries.

medal: A prize given to the winners of a competition. They are often made of metal and worn on a ribbon around the neck.

professional: Earning money from an activity that many people do for fun.

Index